CONGRATULATIONS! YOU ARE GIFTED!

Spiritual Gifts — What Are They?

JIM BURNS / DOUG FIELDS

A practical workbook on Spiritual Gifts
to be used alone or in groups as a study guide.

HARVEST HOUSE PUBLISHERS
EUGENE, OREGON 97402

Dedication

To the youth department at South Coast Community Church . . .

Your input and influence in our lives has been life transforming.

A special thanks to:

Bill and Kathy Starr—You are true friends and "compadres" in ministry.

Community Presbyterian Church Danville youth group for the chance to work through some of these lessons during the summer of 1984.

CONGRATULATIONS! YOU ARE GIFTED!

Copyright © 1986 by Harvest House Publishers
Eugene, Oregon 97402

ISBN 0-89081-478-3

TABLE OF CONTENTS

1. SPIRITUAL GIFTS: ARE THEY FOR EVERYONE?

"Gifted? Who, me? You've got to be kidding."

Yes, you are gifted by God.

> **You are an unrepeatable miracle.**
>
> **You have gifts and potential that are untapped.**
>
> **God can use you to help change the world.**

There may be times when you do not feel very gifted, but the **fact** is that as a Christian you have received spiritual gifts designed especially for you by God.

A spiritual gift is a special ability God gives believers through His Holy Spirit to use for God's glory and purpose.

There are four passages in the New Testament that teach us about these spiritual gifts. Read each passage of Scripture and write the various gifts under each section. Keep in mind Paul's desire for Christians concerning spiritual gifts. *"Now concerning spiritual gifts, brethren, I do not want you to be uninformed"* (1 Cor. 12:1 RSV).

	1 Corinthians 12:4-11			
Romans 12:6-8	**1 Corinthians 12:28-30**		**Ephesians 4:7,8,11,12**	**1 Peter 4:9-11**
1.	1.	8.	1.	1.
2.	2.	9.	2.	2.
3.	3.	10.	3.	3.
4.	4.	11.	4.	
5.	5.	12.	5.	
6.	6.			
7.	7.			

In God's creative workmanship He designs each person to be remarkably different from all others. He also gives a variety of gifts to each individual. No one person has all of the gifts and at the same time there are NO ungifted Christians.

Read and summarize 1 Peter 4:10. Explain how your gifts are to be used:

Read 1 Corinthians 12:4-12.

Why are there many kinds of spiritual gifts?

How do spiritual gifts benefit others and accomplish God's work?

Read 1 Corinthians 12:12-26 and paraphrase Paul's thought:

What would happen to the Body of Christ if everyone had the same gifts?

Keep in mind that as you work through the chapters in this workbook you will begin to learn which gifts God has entrusted to you. Here are four steps to help you find your spiritual gifts:

1. Experiment: Sometimes the only way to know if God has gifted you in a certain area is to try out the gift. You will never know if you have the gift of teaching unless you try to teach!

2. Examine your feelings: Your feelings are very important! If you experiment with the gift of teaching and feel extremely uncomfortable and embarrassed, then perhaps you don't have the gift (at this time). On the other hand, if you were to experiment with the gift of hospitality and found that you enjoy entertaining people, sheltering them, and feeding needy neighbors and, furthermore, if you receive personal joy, satisfaction, and feel used by God doing these things, then you most likely have the gift of hospitality.

3. Evaluate your effectiveness: Every once in a while stop and think about your effectiveness. Ask yourself these three questions: "Am I effective?" "Am I having a worthwhile impact on these people?" "Is God using me in this particular area?" Remember: God has given everyone a gift that will be effective.

4. Expect confirmation from the Body of Christ: Other Christians should be encouraging or discouraging you (with love) in what you do. Listen to them. Weigh their input against your response to the three questions in step three. The Body of Christ is designed to help its members. Find a significant person or group of people in your life who will help you understand and confirm your gifts.

2. TAKING TIME TO CARE

The Gift of Serving

Never forget this: **"The call to Christ is the call to serve!"**

In our generation serving is difficult to incorporate into our life-style. Our culture tells us to "always look out for number one." Yet, for the Christian, being a servant is a necessary ingredient for growth. Even though we are all called to serve, some Christians have the gift of serving.

Perhaps you have the gift of serving! *"We have different gifts, according to the grace given us . . . . Let [each] use it in proportion to his faith. If it is serving, let him serve . . . "* **(Rom. 12:6,7).**

What do you think would happen to the church if no one in the Body exercised the gift of serving?

List roles/tasks within the church that couldn't be done without servants:

The church would be in real trouble if everyone exercised only the gifts that brought attention to themselves.

Leonard Bernstein, the famous orchestra conductor, was asked, "What is the most difficult instrument to play?" He responded:

"Second fiddle. I can get plenty of first violinists, but to find one who plays **second** violin with as much enthusiasm or **second** French horn or **second** flute, now that's a problem. And yet if no one plays second, we have no harmony."[1]

Read Matthew 19:30.

How does this verse relate to the quote about being second fiddle?

What does Jesus mean when He says the "last shall be first"?

Read John 13:1-20.

Why did Jesus wash the disciples' feet?

[1]Charles R. Swindoll, *Improving Your Serve* (Waco: Word Books, 1981), p. 34.

Do you think this attitude of servanthood was a part of the daily life of Jesus? Explain your answer.

Read Philippians 2:3-11.

How does Paul suggest we live our lives according to verses three and four?

What is the central theme of verses five through eight?

What is the result of Christ's obedience and service according to verses nine through eleven?

What specific areas of your life need changing so that you can be more of a servant?

What specific ways can you serve in each of the following areas?

HOME   SCHOOL   CHURCH

Here's a story with an important message:

Shortly after World War II came to close, Europe began picking up the pieces. Much of the Old Country had been ravaged by war and was in ruins. Perhaps the saddest sight of all was that of little orphaned children starving in the streets of those war-torn cities.

Early one chilly morning an American soldier was making his way back to the barracks in London. As he turned the corner in his jeep, he spotted a little lad with his nose pressed to the window of a pastry shop. Inside the cook was kneading dough for a fresh batch of doughnuts. The hungry boy stared in silence, watching every move. The soldier pulled his jeep to the curb, stopped, got out, and walked quietly over to where the little fellow was standing. Through the steamed-up window he could see the mouth-watering morsels as they were being pulled from the oven, piping hot. The boy salivated and released a slight groan as he watched the cook place them onto the glass-enclosed counter ever so carefully.

The soldier's heart went out to the nameless orphan as he stood beside him.

"Son . . . would you like some of those?" The boy was startled.

"Oh, yeah . . . I would!"

The American stepped inside and bought a dozen, put them in a bag, and walked back to where the lad was standing in the foggy cold of the

London morning. He smiled, held out the bag, and said simply:
"Here you are."
As he turned to walk away, he felt a tug on his coat. He looked back and heard the child ask quietly:
"Mister . . . *are you God?*"
We are never more like God than when we give.
"*God so loved the world, that He gave . . . .*"[2]

How does this story speak to you?

SERVICE

On a scale of 1-10 rate your responses to these statements:

1	2	3	4	5	6	7	8	9	10
no		rarely		maybe		sometimes			YES!

I could be described as an "others-centered" person. _____

I enjoy meeting the needs of others. _____

You'll frequently find me volunteering my time to help with the needs of the church. _____

I'm the type of person that likes to reach out to the less fortunate. _____

I feel good when I help with the routine jobs at the church. _____

I feel I have the gift of service. _____

---

[2]Swindoll, *Improving Your Serve* (Waco: Word Books, 1981), pp. 52,53.

The Gift of Helping

"And in the church God has appointed those able to help others" **(1 Cor. 12:28).**

The gift of helping is the special ability to assist others to increase their effectiveness in life. The person with the gift of helps is often a background person who makes things happen without being noticed. Even though this gift is often overlooked, it is a vital act of ministry in the Christian church.

Do you know people with the gift of helps?

Who are they and what do they do?

In Paul's letters he often mentions **faithful helpers.** These helpers were apparently the backbone of the early church.

These faithful helpers freed up Paul and the leaders to do mighty works of ministry. Without the helpers there would have been no Pauls and Peters in the early church.

Read Romans 16:3-6.

What did Priscilla and Aquila do for the Lord?

What is mentioned about Mary in verse 6?

What attitudes or qualities do you feel that a person with the gift of helps needs to have?

Which of these attitudes and qualities would you like to have in your own life?

HELPS

On a scale of 1-10 rate your responses to these statements:

1	2	3	4	5	6	7	8	9	10
no		rarely		maybe		sometimes			YES!

You'll often find me volunteering to do "behind the scenes" activities that few notice but must be done. _____

I'm the one who often cleans up after the meeting without being asked. _____

I seldom think twice before doing a task that might not bring me praise. _____

I receive joy doing jobs that others see as "thankless." _____

I am able to do jobs that others won't do and I feel good about myself. _____

I feel I have the gift of helps. _____

3. ENCOURAGING GOD'S PEOPLE

The Gift of Exhortation

You've probably been around people who have a real gift for encouraging others. They have the unique ability to make you feel special. Their ministry of comfort, challenge, and counsel helps and heals discouraged people.

The word exhortation means "to come alongside." Exhorting someone is coming alongside that person for the sake of encouraging and advising them. The spiritual gift of encouragement does not mean just being able to cheer someone up. Sometimes the most encouraging words are hard to hear because they show us where we are wrong. Even this element of exhortation helps to redirect, clarify, and challenge us.

Do you know someone who has the gift of exhortation? Who?

What are the qualities or characteristics that help you to see that he or she has this special gift?

The apostle Paul had the gift of exhortation. As you read the Book of Acts you will see that Paul was an encouragement to others even after facing brutal beatings, mobs, and imprisonment.

How did Paul use his gift of exhortation in these Scripture passages?

Acts 14:21,22

Acts 20:17-35

Another New Testament Christian who stands out as possessing the gift of exhortation is Barnabas. In fact, everywhere Barnabas appears in the Bible he is encouraging someone.

According to Acts 4:36, what does the name Barnabas mean?

Read Acts 11:19-26.

How was Barnabas an encouragement to the believers in Antioch? (List several ways.)

How was Barnabas an encouragement to Paul in Acts 9:27? (You might need to read the entire account of Paul's conversion in chapter nine for a clearer understanding.)

Barnabas and Paul left the church in Antioch and began to preach around the world (Acts 13). On their first long trip Barnabas wanted to take his nephew John (called Mark) whom Barnabas saw as a potential Christian leader. (Barnabas saw and encouraged potential in people.) John Mark didn't make it through the entire trip and left to return to Jerusalem (Acts 13:13).

After the first trip was completed, Paul and Barnabas decided to go back to visit the places they had been (see Acts 15:36). Again Barnabas wanted to take John Mark but Paul insisted they shouldn't take him since he deserted them earlier. A sharp disagreement broke out. Paul thought of the work; Barnabas thought of the man (see Acts 15:37-41).

Read Acts 15:36-41.

What was the result of the argument? (Acts 15:39,40)

If you were Paul, would you have given John Mark a second chance? Why or why not?

What characteristics made Barnabas a good friend?

We might be missing half of the New Testament books had Barnabas not used his gift of encouragement. Although Barnabas never wrote a book in the New Testament, Paul wrote 13 and Mark wrote one—and Barnabas encouraged them both!

We are commanded in the Scriptures to encourage others even if we do not possess this particular gift. Encouragement is a positive factor for change.

EXHORTATION

On a scale of 1-10 rate your responses to these statements:

1	2	3	4	5	6	7	8	9	10
no		rarely		maybe			sometimes		YES!

I am known for the way I encourage others. _____

I feel I have the ability to comfort those who are "off track" and help them get back on track. _____

I have a desire to learn more about counseling so I can help others. _____

I have helped others in their struggles. _____

I enjoy seeing people respond to encouragement. _____

I feel I have the gift of encouragement. _____

4. GIVING IT AWAY

The Gift of Giving

When we think of giving, whether it be our money, our time, or our talents, all kinds of thoughts run through our minds: "I don't make enough money to give—I can't make it on my allowance." "I'm too busy." "I don't want to." Money can be an especially sensitive area for us. Most people will do just about anything for money; money speaks—LOUDLY. Money has a powerful effect on people. But as Christians we must remember that God is the giver of our material blessings and that all Christians are called to give. Some have the gift of giving.

The gift of giving is the special ability that God gives to certain members of the Body of Christ to contribute their material resources to the work of the Lord with liberality and cheerfulness.[1]

Read 2 Corinthians 8:1-7.

(verse 2) 1. Were the Macedonian people wealthy?

(verse 2) 2. What did they have in place of money?

(verse 3) 3. How much did they give?

(verse 4) 4. What was their attitude in giving?

(verse 5) 5. Why do you suppose they had such a good attitude about giving?

[1]C. Peter Wagner, *Your Spiritual Gifts Can Help Your Church Grow* (Ventura: Regal Books, 1979), p. 96.

Paul explains the gift this way:

> *"And since we have gifts that differ according to the grace given to us, . . . he who gives, with liberality"* **(Rom. 12:6-8 NASB).**

Another interpretation says:

> *"If God has given you money, be generous . . . "* **(Rom. 12:8 TLB).**

Here are some principles to help you become a better giver:

Attitude Check #1: Give without boasting.

Read Matthew 6:3,4.

Why do you think we should give in secret?

Attitude Check #2: Give with a proper perspective.

Read 1 Timothy 6:10.

This often-misquoted passage doesn't say "money is the root of all evil" but "the *love* of money is a root of all kinds of evil."

What is the danger of loving money?

What unhealthy attitudes show up in people who live for money?

Attitude Check #3: Give sacrificially.

Read Mark 12:41-44.

Why was the widow honored more than the rich people?

Why was this important to Jesus?

Attitude Check #4: Give what you have.

Read Luke 12:48b.

What does Jesus mean when He says, "From everyone who has been given much, much will be demanded" (NIV)?

Read 1 Timothy 6:17-19.

What does God require of a rich person?

Are you rich? Think about this question as you read this poem.

"I asked God for strength that I might achieve.
I was made weak that I might learn humbly to obey.

I asked God for health that I might do greater things.
I was given infirmity that I might do better things.

I asked for riches that I might be happy.
I was given poverty that I might be wise.

I asked for power that I might have the praise of men.
I was given weakness that I might feel the need of God.

I asked for all things that I might enjoy life.
I was given life that I might enjoy all things.

I got nothing I asked for
but everything I had hoped for . . .

Almost despite myself my unspoken prayers were answered.

I am among all men most richly blessed."

Unknown Confederate Soldier[2]

God has a purpose in giving

Before reading the following verses, answer this question: Why do you think God wants us to give?

---

[2]Tim Hansel, *When I Relax, I Feel Guilty* (Elgin: David C. Cook Publishers, 1979), p. 89.

Read Acts 20:35.

What is the meaning of this simple yet profound statement?

The church often tends to focus on the more glamorous or controversial gifts. But where would our pastors and teachers be without the support of those who give?

"Remember this: Whoever sows sparingly will also reap sparingly, and whoever sows generously will also reap generously. Each man should give what he has decided in his heart to give, not reluctantly or under compulsion, for God loves a cheerful giver. And God is able to make all grace abound to you, so that in all things at all times, having all that you need, you will abound in every good work"
(2 Cor. 9:6-8 NIV).

What is the *attitude* of the giver to be?

How will the giver reap plenty?

What is God's promise to the giver?

One by one He took them from me
    All the things I valued most;
'Til I was empty-handed,
    Every glittering toy was lost.
And I walked earth's highways, grieving,
    In my rags and poverty.
Until I heard His voice inviting,
    "Lift those empty hands to Me!"

Then I turned my hands toward heaven,
    And He filled them with a store
Of His own transcendent riches,
    'Til they could contain no more.

And at last I comprehended
    With my stupid mind, and dull
That God cannot pour His riches
    Into hands already full.

                Source Unknown[3]

How does this poem relate to the gift of giving?

---

[3]Charles R. Swindoll, *Improving Your Serve* (Waco: Word Books, 1981), pp. 190,191.

GIVING

On a scale of 1-10 rate your responses to these statements:

1	2	3	4	5	6	7	8	9	10
no		rarely		maybe		sometimes			YES!

I see myself as a person who is very generous when it comes to giving money to my church.

_____

I enjoy giving money to the needy.

_____

I have a strong desire to use my money wisely, knowing God will direct my giving.

_____

I am a cheerful giver of my money.

_____

I am confident that God will take care of my needs when I give sacrificially and cheerfully.

_____

I feel I have the gift of giving.

_____

5. BUILDING UP THE CHURCH

The Gift of Teaching

There are some teachers who have a remarkable impact on our lives. Usually it is not so much **what** they teach as **how** they teach. These teachers have been given a special gift to make spiritual truth and other subjects come alive. Many of these teachers have used this gift to greatly influence our lives.

"So we are to use our different gifts in accordance with the grace that God has given us . . . . if it is to teach we should teach" **(Rom. 12:6,7 TEV).**

List a few of your favorite teachers and what you have learned from them (Sunday School, public school, other).

TEACHER   WHAT I LEARNED

What are a few things teachers can do to make the Christian faith more relevant?

What are a few ways of teaching outside of a classroom setting?

The gift of teaching can be displayed in many ways: teaching children, peers, adults, small groups, large groups, in the church, in the school system, in the United States, in Africa, etc. List all the different varieties of teaching you can think of. Circle the settings where you feel you would be comfortable teaching.

Of the types of teaching you circled, which *one* makes you feel most secure, comfortable, and confident?

Read and paraphrase James 3:1.

Why do you think the words of James 3:1 are so harsh?

TEACHING

On a scale of 1-10 rate your responses to these statements:

1	2	3	4	5	6	7	8	9	10
no		rarely		maybe		sometimes			YES!

I enjoy explaining biblical truths to people. _____

I think I have what it takes to teach a Bible study or lead a small group discussion. _____

I am willing to spend extra time studying biblical principles in order to communicate them clearly to others. _____

Because of my teaching, I have brought others to a better understanding of the Christian faith. _____

Others tell me I present the Gospel in a way that is easy to understand. _____

I feel I have the gift of teaching. _____

The Gift of Pastoring

Throughout the different church denominations many different words are used for pastor: minister, elder, priest, preacher, and others. But the term pastor has a significant meaning.

"And his gifts were that some should be . . . pastors" **(Eph. 4:11 RSV).**

Pastor is the Latin word for *shepherd.*

Read John 10:11-16.

What qualities of a shepherd are described in this parable of Jesus?

If you were a shepherd, what would be your main responsibility?

What did Jesus mean when He said to Peter, "Take care of my sheep" (John 21:16 NIV)?

What else does the Bible say about the act of shepherding? Read the following Scriptures and next to the verse write the key words or phrases that lead to a better understanding of shepherding.

Hebrews 13:20

1 Peter 2:25

Acts 20:28

Can you see how the New Testament portrays the shepherd as the person who cares for the flock and leads them into safe places? If the sheep wander away the shepherd seeks them out and saves them. He protects them from their enemies.

How would you define "pastor" if the word pastor comes from shepherd?

How can you "pastor" your friends?

List three friends and some specific action you could take to shepherd, pastor, and care for each of them this week.

MY FRIENDS   MY ACTION STEPS

1.

2.

3.

PASTORING

On a scale of 1-10 rate your responses to these statements:

1	2	3	4	5	6	7	8	9	10
no		rarely		maybe		sometimes			YES!

I have a way of relating to and comforting those who have fallen away from the Lord.   _____

I try to know people in a personal way so that we feel comfortable with one another.   _____

I would like the responsibilities that my pastor has.   _____

I can see myself taking responsibility for the spiritual growth of others.   _____

When I teach from the Bible my concern is that I see results in the spiritual growth of others.   _____

I would like to be a pastor.   _____

6. THE OPEN HEART

The Gift of Mercy

The gift of mercy is a gift that gets little recognition yet has great personal rewards.

"And since we have gifts that differ according to the grace given us . . . . he who shows mercy let him exercise his gift with cheerfulness" **(Rom. 12:6,8 NASB).**

To have mercy means to be kind or compassionate. It means to relieve suffering. *Webster's Dictionary* defines mercy as "the quality in something experienced or observed which arouses feelings of pity, sorrow, sympathy, or compassion."[1]

The gift of mercy may be demonstrated by direct personal involvement with the sick, outcast, poor, aged, mentally ill, deformed, hungry, shut-in, retarded, deprived, widowed, sad, underprivileged, alcoholic, or handicapped. A person with the gift of mercy wants intensely to meet the needs of those who hurt.

Read Luke 10:30-37.

What specific acts of mercy did the Samaritan perform?

This man not only felt sorry—he ACTED!

In the Book of Acts a jailer became a Christian in the presence of Paul and Silas. What acts of mercy did this jailer do to help Paul and Silas? (Acts 16:33,34.)

---

[1]*Webster's New World Dictionary* (The World Publishing Co., 1966).

What do you think are the areas of greatest need in your community? in the world?

What achievable steps could you take to show mercy in these areas?

Will you commit yourself to acting with mercy toward one of these needs? Which one? What will you do?

MERCY

On a scale of 1-10 rate your responses to these statements:

1	2	3	4	5	6	7	8	9	10
no		rarely		maybe		sometimes			YES!

I enjoy giving hope to those in need (such as the lonely, elderly, or shut-ins). _____

I would like to have a ministry with those who are needy. _____

I would like to visit rest or comfort homes and other institutions where people need visitors. _____

I am very compassionate to those in need. _____

I have a desire to work with people who have special physical needs. _____

I feel I have the gift of mercy. _____

The Gift of Hospitality

If you enjoy organizing and hosting a party, making strangers feel welcome, or sharing with those in need, you may have the gift of hospitality.

"Practice hospitality" (Rom. 12:13 RSV).

"Practice hospitality ungrudgingly to one another" (1 Pet. 4:9 RSV).

Look up the verses below and list the name of the person who was hospitable and what he or she did.

Acts 9:43

Acts 16:15

Acts 16:34

In the days of Jesus and in the days of the early church, people were dependent on others for food and lodging as they traveled from city to city. Do you think there is still a need for the gift of hospitality today with all the motels and hotels that are available to travelers? Explain your thoughts.

Whether you have the gift of hospitality or not, what can you do to develop a stronger attitude of hospitality?

Read 1 Peter 4:9.

Why do you think Paul adds "ungrudgingly or without complaint" when he speaks of being hospitable?

If you know someone with the gift of hospitality, why not write them a short note today expressing your gratitude for their generosity?

HOSPITALITY

On a scale of 1-10 rate your responses to these statements:

1	2	3	4	5	6	7	8	9	10
no		**rarely**		**maybe**		**sometimes**			**YES!**

When people are in need I enjoy having them in my home. I do not feel like they are intruding.

_____

I enjoy having strangers in my home. I like making them feel comfortable.

_____

I feel like God has given me the ability to make others feel comfortable in my home.

_____

I enjoy providing food and housing to those in need.

_____

I want my house to always be a spot where people in need can come and find rest.

_____

I feel I have the gift of hospitality.

_____

7. KNOWING WHERE TO GO

The Gift of Leadership

Many times when we hear the word "leader" we think of an authority figure standing above everyone else. He or she might have an outgoing personality or the ability to speak well in front of groups. But these qualities do not always make a person a good leader.

Even if you are shy and timid you may have real leadership ability. Perhaps you are a leader but you've never realized it.

To help shatter some of our misconceptions, let's take a look at Timothy. Notice how Paul encouraged Timothy in the following verses. After each verse write the advice that Paul gave to Timothy concerning Timothy's leadership.

1 Timothy 4:12

1 Timothy 6:14

2 Timothy 4:6,7

2 Timothy 2:22-26

Read Philippians 2:19-22.

How does Paul describe Timothy to the Philippians?

"And since we have gifts that differ according to the grace given to us, let each exercise them accordingly . . . . He who leads, with diligence" **(Rom. 12:6,8 NASB).**

The literal definition of a leader is one who "stands before" others. This means the gift of leadership is the special ability from God to set goals from God and then lead others to work together to carry out those goals for the glory of God.

List a few qualities of a leader that would support this definition.

Jesus Christ gives us a perfect model of leadership. From what you know of the life of Jesus, can you recall specific times when Jesus used the gift of leadership?

Jesus appointed, trained, and led 12 men (His apostles) who, after Christ's death, became the leaders of the early church (Acts 4:37; 9:27). During Christ's time with these men, He taught them many things, including leadership. Two of Christ's apostles, James and John, asked Him an interesting question.

Read Mark 10:35-41.
What was their question?

Do you think they asked that question because:

a. They always wanted to be close to Jesus?

b. They thought since they were leaders they should be first in God's kingdom?

c. They thought those were the best seats in the "house"?

d. Other

Explain your answer.

Let's see how Jesus responded to their question:

"So Jesus called them all together to him and said, 'You know that the men who are considered rulers of the heathen have power over them, and the leaders have complete authority. This, however, is not the way it is among you. If one of you wants to be great, he must be the servant of the rest; and if one of you wants to be first, he must be the slave of all. For even the Son of Man did not come to be served; he came to serve and give his life to redeem many people'" **(Mark 10:42-45 TEV).**

What point is Jesus trying to make in these verses?

What should the words "leader" and "servant" mean to a Christian? How does this differ from the meaning the world attaches to these words?

Read John 13:1-17.

Was Jesus portraying leadership qualities when He washed His disciples' feet?

Jesus not only demonstrated that leaders are to be servants, but also that they are to be examples to others.

Do you know someone who fits the description of a servant as demonstrated by Jesus? (They don't have to be leaders.)

What "servant qualities" does this person display?

LEADERSHIP

On a scale of 1-10 rate your responses to these statements:

1	2	3	4	5	6	7	8	9	10
no		rarely		maybe		sometimes			YES!

I feel I know where I am going (and other people seem to follow). _____

I would enjoy leading, inspiring, and motivating others to become involved in God's work. _____

I want to lead people to the best solution when they have troubles. _____

I have influenced others to complete a task or to find a biblical answer that helped their lives. _____

When I'm in a group I'm usually the leader or I take the lead if no one else does. _____

I feel like I have leadership skills. _____

The Gift of Administration

The gift of administration is very similar to the gift of leadership. These gifts have been described as different from each other, but they are related. The difference is that leadership is defined by what a person **is** while administration is defined by what the person **does.**

"And God has appointed in the church . . . administrators" **(1 Cor. 12:28 RSV).**

The Greek word Paul used that has been translated "administrators" is a graphic word that literally refers to the work of a helmsman or pilot (captain) who steers a ship through rocks and sandbars to safe harbor.

The gift of administration is the special ability that God gives to certain members of the Body of Christ which helps them to clearly understand the present and future goals of a group. People with the gift of administration are able to plan workable ways to reach these goals.

How does this differ from the gift of leadership?

A _____ could be thought of as a quarterback who helps the football team score a touchdown. While the _____ is like a coach who designs the plays for the quarterback to run.

The visit of Jethro to his son-in-law Moses is recorded in Exodus 18. Jethro used his gift of administration to greatly help the ministry of Moses.

43

Read Exodus 18:13-27.

What advice did Jethro give to Moses?

How did this advice affect the life and work of Moses?

What could someone with the gift of administration do to help the church? Your youth group?

Church:

Youth Group:

Can a leader also have the gift of administration?

What positive steps should the leader take if he or she doesn't have the gift of administration?

ADMINISTRATION

On a scale of 1-10 rate your responses to these statements:

1	2	3	4	5	6	7	8	9	10
no		rarely		maybe		sometimes			YES!

I see clearly that a job can be done more effectively if I allow others to assist. _____

I would enjoy directing a vacation Bible school, recreation program, or special event for my church. _____

I can give others responsibilities for a task or project and help them accomplish it. _____

I am able to set goals and plan the most effective way to reach them. _____

I feel I have the gift of administration. _____

8. DISCOVERING THE RIGHT PATH

The Gift of Wisdom

Have you ever met a person who was unusually wise? For some reason certain people have the ability to give solid counsel. Their insight into difficult problems is absolutely brilliant. These people probably have the gift of wisdom. Although the Bible challenges all of us to pursue wisdom, there are some people who have an exceptional ability to "see clearly." Their opinions are highly respected.

"For to one is given the word of wisdom through the Spirit" **(1 Cor. 12:6 NASB).**

James 3:17 draws a picture of godly wisdom. List below the qualities of wisdom given in this verse.

Which of these qualities of wisdom would you most like to work on this week? What specific steps could you take to develop this quality in your life?

The Book of Proverbs (also called **Wisdom Literature**) is filled with descriptive illustrations of wisdom. Read Proverbs 2:1-12. Then, answer the following questions.

According to verses 1-5 what steps are required before you can gain wisdom?

What significance does verse six have in helping you understand wisdom?

Read verses seven to nine. What does God do for those who receive His wisdom?

List the results of allowing wisdom to enter your life according to Proverbs 2:10-12.

RESULTS

(verse 10) 1.

2.

(verse 11) 1.

2.

(verse 12) 1.

WISDOM

On a scale of 1-10 rate your responses to these statements:

1	2	3	4	5	6	7	8	9	10
no		rarely		maybe		sometimes			YES!

My friends view me as a person who is wise.   _____

I feel God has given me the ability to make wise decisions.   _____

God has given me the ability to give clear counsel and advice to others.   _____

I feel confident that my decisions are in harmony with God's will.   _____

I usually see clear solutions to complicated problems.   _____

I feel God has blessed me with the gift of wisdom.   _____

The Gift of Knowledge

The biblical gift of knowledge has little or nothing to do with your IQ. The gift of knowledge has been defined as the ability to understand truth that is unknown by natural means.

"For to one is given the word of wisdom through the Spirit" **(2 Cor. 12:8 NASB).**

Read 2 Samuel 12:1-14.

How did Nathan know of David's sin?

What was God's purpose for Nathan confronting David?

How could the gift of knowledge benefit the Body of Christ? your church?

Here's an illustration:

> A small factory had to stop operations when an essential piece of machinery broke down. When none of the factory personnel could get it operating again, an outside expert was called in. After looking over the situation for a minute, the expert took a hammer and gently tapped the machine on a certain spot, and it immediately started running again. When he submitted his bill for $100, the plant supervisor went into a rage and demanded an itemized bill. It read as follows: "For hitting the machine, $1; for knowing where to hit it, $99."[1]

It is essential in the church today that we have people who "know where to hit." These people are not necessarily needed to fix machinery, but rather for the important work of making crucial decisions. God may also use people with the gift of knowledge as Christian scholars to research, interpret, and investigate His Word so that people may understand it more clearly.

Who do you know who might have this gift?

How have they been a help to you?

---

[1]Kenneth O. Gaugel, *Unwrap Your Spiritual Gifts* (Wheaton: Victor Books, 1983), p. 62.

KNOWLEDGE

On a scale of 1-10 rate your responses to these statements:

1	2	3	4	5	6	7	8	9	10
no		rarely		maybe		sometimes			YES!

I have expressed thoughts of truth that have given insight to others. _____

I desire to fully understand biblical truths. _____

I am able to help others understand God's Word. _____

I tend to use biblical insights when I share with others. _____

I have the ability to learn new insights on my own. _____

I feel I have the gift of knowledge. _____

9. SHARING THE GOOD NEWS

The Gift of Evangelism

The word evangelist appears only three times in the entire New Testament (Acts 21:8, Eph. 4:11 and 2 Tim. 4:5).

In Ephesians 4:11 we read, *"He gave some to be . . . evangelists"* **(NIV).**

Though the word isn't used many times, its meaning is clearly defined. It means one who proclaims the Good News.

Read Matthew 28:16-20.

Why do you think this Scripture passage is often called "The Great Commission"?

According to this Scripture, what are the important elements of the Great Commission?

Read Acts 1:8.

Do you think this verse applies to us today?

According to this verse, who empowers us to go and share the Good News?

The Bible tells us that Philip was an evangelist (see Acts 21:8). Read Acts 8:4-8 and list the actions of Philip and the actions of the crowd.

The job of an evangelist is not to nurture Christians but rather to preach to unbelievers the message of salvation in Christ.

What was Philip's message?

Acts 8:12

Acts 8:35

What kind of results did Philip get?

Acts 8:6

Acts 8:12

If your life has been changed by Christ, you are a new creation (see 2 Cor. 5:17) and you have something to share.

With whom can you share the Good News of Christ?

How can you share the Good News with this person? (Examples: go out to lunch, bring to church, etc.)

In the space below write the name of a fellow Christian who could hold you accountable to this goal.

From what you have learned what differences do you see between the gift of evangelism and the gift of pastor?

EVANGELISM

On a scale of 1-10 rate your responses to these statements:

1	2	3	4	5	6	7	8	9	10
no		rarely		maybe		sometimes			YES!

I can tell nonbelievers about my relationship with Christ in a comfortable manner. _____

I always think of new ways in which I can share Christ with my nonbelieving friends. _____

I have the ability to direct conversations toward the message of Christ. _____

I have led others to a personal relationship with Christ. _____

I desire to learn more about God so I can share Him in a clearer way. _____

I feel I have the gift of evangelism. _____

The Gift of Prophecy

When the word "prophet" is spoken we often think of prediction of future events, fortune-telling, predicting the outcome of a football game, or some other form of gaining truth that was previously unknown to us!

The Old Testament prophets acted as God's mouthpiece for speaking His message to kings, common people, and entire nations. The messages they spoke usually pertained to future events. In the New Testament and in recent history, prophecy, which in Greek means "to speak forth," usually has a different meaning. In the church the gift of prophecy is the ability to "speak forth" or "proclaim" God's truth and how that truth applies to our everyday life.

"But one who prophesies, preaching the messages of God, is helping others grow in the Lord, encouraging and comforting them" **(1 Cor. 14:3 TLB).**

According to the following Scriptures, what seems to be the primary job of a New Testament prophet?

1 Corinthians 14:3

Acts 15:32

Read Acts 13:1-5.

What were the responsibilities of Barnabas and Saul?

Paul stresses the importance of the gift of prophecy in 1 Corinthians 14.

Read 1 Corinthians 14:1-5,39.

Why do you think Paul views prophecy as being so important?

What issues do you think a person with the gift of prophecy would speak on in the 20th century?

Do you know someone who has the gift of prophecy? If so, how do they make you feel when you hear them speak?

PROPHECY

On a scale of 1-10 rate your responses to these statements:

1	2	3	4	5	6	7	8	9	10
no		rarely		maybe		sometimes			YES!

I have given others important messages at the perfect time that
I felt came from God.   _____

I feel I have the ability to reveal God's truth about the future.   _____

I desire to speak messages from God that will challenge people to
change.   _____

I have had the chance to proclaim God's truth at the required time.   _____

I have given messages that were judgments from God.   _____

I feel I have the gift of prophecy.   _____

10. SEARCHING FOR A SIGN

The Gift of Tongues and The Interpretation of Tongues

"To one there is given through the Spirit . . . the ability to speak in different kinds of tongues, and to still another the interpretation of tongues" (1 Cor. 12:8,10).

In the Christian faith, speaking in tongues and the interpretation of tongues are perhaps the most widely debated and misunderstood gifts of the Spirit. Some say speaking in tongues is not a gift, others say it is a gift. Some say the gift was for the first century, others believe tongues to be evidence of the baptism of the Holy Spirit. Let's investigate what the Bible has to say about this interesting gift so we can begin to develop our own opinion on the subject.*

What is the gift of tongues?

It is evident that in the early church many men and women spoke in tongues. Read the following verses and summarize your impression of these Scripture references.

Acts 2:1-13

Acts 10:44-46

Acts 19:1-7

* We strongly believe that as you study this chapter you should talk with a leader from your church for wisdom and insight on this subject. Please note that we cannot attempt to provide in the limited space available a thorough study of these particular gifts.

Read 1 Corinthians 14:2.

What do you think is the significance of this verse?

What is the purpose of the gift of tongues?

Let's look at three purposes given in the New Testament.

A. A Sign

Read Acts 2 and 1 Corinthians 14:22.

To whom is the sign directed?

What is the purpose of the sign?

B. Edification (building up of the Body of Christ)

Read 1 Corinthians 14:4. Who is edified?

Read 1 Corinthians 14:5. Who is edified when speaking in tongues is interpreted? (also see 14:26)

Read 1 Corinthians 14:13-19 and summarize what this Scripture teaches about the gift of tongues and the interpretation of tongues.

C. Prayer

Read 1 Corinthians 14:4. Do you think speaking in tongues is a form of prayer?

What are the biblical guidelines?

Paul gave the church at Corinth instructions for speaking in tongues. He wanted to make it quite clear that the gift of tongues was no greater gift than the other gifts of the Spirit.

Read 1 Corinthians 14. List Paul's rules:

(verse 26) 1.

(verse 27) 2.

(verses 27,28) 3.

(verses 33,40) 4.

From what you have learned, what are your present thoughts about speaking in tongues?

TONGUES

On a scale of 1-10 rate your responses to these statements:

1	2	3	4	5	6	7	8	9	10
no		rarely		maybe		sometimes			YES!

I believe I have a prayer language which is in a tongue unknown to me. _____

I have spoken in tongues. _____

When I speak in tongues, I feel God's Spirit within me. _____

Others have interpreted my unknown prayer language. _____

An unknown language comes to me when I'm at a loss for words in my prayer time. _____

I feel I have the gift of tongues. _____

The Gift of Healing

At one time or another we have all prayed for healing, either for ourselves or for a loved one. We've heard of miraculous healings and we've also known times when it was apparent that God did not answer our prayer for a healing. Yet the Bible does speak of the gift of healing and the Gospels as well as the Book of Acts are filled with miraculous healings from God.

"There are different kinds of gifts, but that one Spirit . . . . To another gifts of healing by that one Spirit" **(1 Cor. 12:4,9 NIV).**

Read the verses below and write down the person who had the gift of healing and what or who they healed. (This is not a complete list.)

Matthew 9:35

Acts 3:2-8

Acts 8:6-8

Acts 14:8-10

List the steps given in James 5:14-16 for healing the sick.

Let's look at another type of healing: **emotional healing.**

"The Spirit of the Lord is upon me, because he hath anointed me to preach the gospel to the poor; he hath sent me to heal the broken hearted, to preach deliverance to the captives, and recovering of sight to the blind, to set at liberty them that are bruised . . . " **(Luke 4:18, KJV).**

The word translated "brokenhearted" refers to those who are emotionally and mentally shattered. In fact, the last phrase of this quotation, "to set at liberty them that are bruised," also refers to emotional healing.

Could it be possible that emotional healing might be as important to our understanding of healing as physical healing? Why or why not?

What occupations are directed at emotional healing?

How might the gift of healing be demonstrated in people in these occupations?

In the Bible there is another form of healing called **spiritual healing.**

Read Matthew 13:14,15.

How could the prophecy from Isaiah refer to spiritual healing?

Read this statement found in 1 Peter 2:24: *"Christ himself carried our sins in his body to the cross, so that we might die to sin and live for righteousness. It is by his wounds that you have been healed"* **(TEV).**

According to this verse, why are we healed?

How does this verse relate to your life?

Write what you perceive the definition of healing to be in light of this information on physical, emotional, and spiritual healing.

Whether or not you have the gift of healing, what can you be doing to help heal people with physical, emotional, and spiritual needs?

Complete this sentence: I may not have the God-given gift of physical healing, but I can attempt to heal others by . . .

The Gift of Miracles

Scattered throughout the Bible are incredible illustrations of miracles: the parting of the Red Sea for Moses and the people of Israel, Elijah breathing life into the widow's dead son, Jesus turning water into wine, Jesus walking on water, and more. Sometimes the miracles of the Bible seem distant when we look at them from the 20th century. Let's investigate this gift to see if it is for today.

"There are different kinds of spiritual gifts . . . to another miraculous powers . . . "
(1 Cor. 12:4,10 NIV).

Read Acts 3:1-12.

Who was healed in this story?

By what power was this man healed?

Why were the people who saw the miracle amazed?

Why was Peter upset by their amazement?

Why do you think God uses miracles?

What are some modern-day miracles?

Miracles are supernatural acts of God used by God for His plan and purpose. Many of us want to see a sign from God before we totally commit to Him. Or we want the clouds to spell out an answer to our prayer so we know God is really on our team.

Read Matthew 12:38.

What did the Pharisees want?

Read Matthew 12:39,40.

How did Christ respond?

Does this mean we should never ask for miracles?

What miracles, if any, have taken place in your own life?

What miracles would you like to take place in your life?

MIRACLES

On a scale of 1-10 rate your responses to these statements:

1	2	3	4	5	6	7	8	9	10
no		rarely		maybe		sometimes			YES!

God has used me in a supernatural way to heal someone. _____

I have healed a handicapped person. _____

Many incredible acts of God have happened to others through me. _____

I have the ability to heal. _____

God is glorified when He heals others through me. _____

I feel I have the gift of miracles/healing. _____

11. ADVENTUROUS FAITH

The Gift of Faith

"To one is given . . . faith by the same Spirit" **(1 Cor. 12:8,9 RSV).**

Have you ever met a person with extraordinary faith? Their gift of faith causes them to trust in God for exceptional miracles in addition to their remarkably established risk-taking faith. All Christians are believers by faith yet there are those who from the Bible days to the present day have demonstrated an unusual ability to depend on God.

Let's investigate the faith "Hall of Fame" in the Bible.

Read Hebrews 11.

List each person of faith this chapter mentions and the event associated with his or her great faith.

Why is this such an inspiring chapter?

Define the word faith in your own words using Hebrews 11:1 as a resource.

What eternal truth is found in Hebrews 11:6?

Do you know any modern day people who could be included in the faith "Hall of Fame"? Write their name and faith experience in the space below.

Why is it difficult at times to have faith?

What could you accomplish with your life if you had more faith?

FAITH

On a scale of 1-10 rate your responses to these statements:

1	2	3	4	5	6	7	8	9	10
no		rarely		maybe		sometimes			YES!

I often feel I know God's will even when others aren't sure. _____

I enjoy helping others with spiritual needs. _____

I find it easy to trust in God in difficult situations. _____

I trust in God for supernatural miracles. _____

Others in my group see me as a faithful Christian. _____

I feel I have the gift of faith. _____

The Gift of Apostle

"And his gifts were that some should be apostles" **(Eph. 4:11 RSV).**

To best understand the meaning of apostleship we must look at the first apostles. They were the commissioned "messengers" of the early church. The apostles took the message of the Good News of Jesus Christ to the world. A modern-day apostle is one who feels God's call to take the same message of Jesus Christ to the world. Today we call this person a missionary.

Paul was an apostle and missionary. Read Ephesians 3:1-13.

What was Paul trying to communicate to the Gentiles? (see verse 6)

What title did Paul give himself? (see verse 7)

Because of his title what was Paul able to do? (see verse 8)

What was the goal of his missionary work? (see verses 9-12)

From what you know of Paul, did he accomplish this goal?

What is the meaning of Jesus' statement in Matthew 24:14?

With the incredible needs in our world how do you feel about the following statement?

Young men and women should seriously consider becoming missionaries to our hurting world. God needs people who are willing to teach, preach, do business, and a host of other things in order for God's message to reach the world.

Mark the boxes that describe appropriately your feelings about the above statement.

☐ I feel guilty.

☐ I'm willing to go if God calls.

☐ I'm not the missionary type.

☐ I'm ready to go today.

☐ _____

Write in your feelings.

In the space below write out positive and negative reasons for being a missionary.

POSITIVE   **NEGATIVE**

If you do not have the gift of apostleship or missionary, what can you do to support the work of Christ around the world?

APOSTLE

On a scale of 1-10 rate your responses to these statements:

1	2	3	4	5	6	7	8	9	10
no		rarely		maybe		sometimes			YES!

I feel I could learn a new language well enough to minister to those in a different culture. _____

I feel comfortable when I'm around people of a different culture, race, or language. _____

I adapt easily to a change of settings. _____

I have a strong desire to see people in other countries won to the Lord. _____

I am willing to go wherever God wants to send me. _____

I would like to be a missionary. _____